Eternally You

BRIANNA ELLIS

POEMS

For more information, contact:
Email: Briannae913@gmail.com

ISBN: 979-8-9913540-0-4 (Paperback)
ISBN: 979-8-9913540-2-8 (Hardcover)

First paperback edition printed in 2024.

Front cover art by Polina Raulina
Cover illustrated by Jishan Anik
Edited by Helen B., Ph. D.

DEDICATION

To Sweet Sandra Ellis

This poetry book is dedicated to my dear mother, whose poetic expression has always inspired me. You are the reason I picked up the pen and spoke my heart. I am forever grateful for your love and continuous support.

INTRODUCTION

Eternally You is the expression of our infinite presence and potential. No matter where you are, you will always be you. There is simply no one else like you, and your essence is everlasting. May this poetry book accompany you along your healing journey, as you find peace in nature, stillness, reflection and forgiveness. Your higher self is patiently awaiting your elevation. Unlock endless possibilities, self-love and strength by being Eternally You.

TABLE OF CONTENTS

TABLE OF CONTENTS

Section One

Nature's Beauty

Whenever I find myself praying for abundance, I step outside and realize that it's everywhere around me. Every creature, every plant scattered across this green earth serves a divine purpose. Even inside the smallest molecule of nectar, you will discover God's most mystical creations. Consciousness is eternally implanted in every living thing. Each one holds an infinite energy that transcends time and space. Just planting your feet on God's luscious grass and rich soil ignites healing waves throughout your mind, body and soul. Just as powerful as a full moon gleams above us, every star is a reminder of the luminous universe that exists inside of you. We are one.

Forever Butterfly

Unconsciously in her cocoon,
once wrapped in misery.
A being lived uncomfortably,
before deciding to break free.

This stubborn butterfly took flight,
and battled skies with battered wings.
She didn't recognize her beauty.
She thrived at bumping into things.

"Why should I stop to smell the flowers?"
The bitter butterfly had questioned.
She blotted out her pretty colors-
a false sense of self-protection.
So, she ignored the bliss of nature
and avoided her reflection.
Until an angel landed in her life
and welcomed a connection.

The butterfly was quickly startled,
"How could I be loved for me?
It's been so long, I don't know who I am."
She panicked endlessly.
This angel pacified the butterfly
and loved her patiently.
Assured her of pure inner beauty,
even when she disagreed.

Self-sabotage was once the norm,
until the butterfly transformed.
She slowly stepped into resiliency,
and weathered every storm.
She was delighted by new textures.
Her precious colors reappeared!
The butterfly engulfed in nature
and laughed at everything she feared.

The butterfly glides blissfully.
Her wings now gleam with gratitude.
Guided by her grateful attitude,
blessings grew in magnitude.

The Irony of Stillness

Stillness in the mind
is a powerful gem to find.
I release and feel at ease,
as I mentally unwind.

When I took a look inside
and finally sat with myself,
I realized that peace of mind
is more valuable than wealth.

Now, I'm embracing nature's beauty,
gratefully on evening strolls.
Joyous sounds of birds chirping
is God speaking to my soul.
Rays of sunshine stain the pavement.
Squirrels scatter left and right.
Though my mind is settled peacefully,
my heart has taken flight.

Elevated by abundance,
marveled by greenery.
Stillness is transformative,
it changed my scenery.

A sound mind unlocks the world.
My heart and soul will remain open.
Who would've known that restful thoughts
create a lifestyle full of motion?

Stories of Houseplants

My houseplants
whisper stories
of inconsistency.
Tall snake plants slither
while Peace Lillies wither.
Hard to please,
never truly at peace.
Why do they die
from too much light?
Shouldn't everybody
love the sunshine?

Droopy leaves
and burnt edges
are snipped away
on bad days.
Under-watered.
Overstimulated.
Reflected corners
of my mind.
I try and try,
but still
the soil
feels so dry.
Cool and damp,
sometimes.
Filling my cup
along this quest
to find the light.

My houseplants
whisper stories
of inconsistency.
But still we
try and try,
tenaciously.
Ever-growing,
painfully.
Yet patiently,
We thrive in light
and trust in love,
we will survive.

Moonlight Queen

Her melanin glistens
in the shadows of nightfall.
Kissed by the cosmos,
the Moonlight Queen.

Her dark complexion shimmers,
beneath a symphony of stars.
She is royalty:
the Moonlight Queen.

Slivers of the universe
reside in her eyes.
Coupled with her crescent smile,
the Moonlight Queen.

Her aura exudes
a soulful sensation
inside her constellation,
the Moonlight Queen.

The moon orbits her Afro,
Glowing and flowing.
For all eternity, I'll be
the Moonlight Queen.

Her Mysteries

Majestically,
Infinitely,
she's the epitome
of mystery.
Her sacred synchronicities,
designed by His divinity.

Reminds me of my melanin.
Her earthly glow
flows from within.
Her royal rays
kiss chocolate skin.
Mahogany shades
glistening.
Absorbing light,
she exudes love.
Afros resemble
boxwood shrubs.

I see myself
inside her roots.
Her ancient womb
bears sacred fruits.
Deeply embedded
as Baobab trees.
Her heavenly breeze
keeps me at ease.
Handcrafted by
the Most High God,
she's blossoming for centuries.

Forever flourishing,
always nourishing.
Her flowers bloom,
we are in tune.
I look inside myself and see
Mother Nature's mysteries.

Section Two

Love

"Love is green. Love is nurturing. Love is supreme. Love is eternal. Love has no limitations. Love is warm. Love is magical. Love quenches my thirst. Love is power. Love is strength. Love is the desire that never ends."

-Dhanshaly Persaud

Love is the pulsating rhythm of our heartbeats. Vibrational waves of warmth, wrapped in unforgettable bliss. Love is a sweet scent and soft lips, planting forehead kisses at moonlight hours. Love is the corners of your smile and gentle hands caressing mine. Love is beauty and grace, powerful yet unconditional. Love is an everlasting energy. Love is life unconfined. Love is our soaring spirits intensified once detached from worldly limits. Love is infinite. Love is universal. Love is the depths of our souls, liberated and joyfully present. Together, we are love.

For My Wife

Visualizations of love
cannot compare to our reality.

You scooped me up so casually,
but knew just how to...
handle me.
Terminating my toxicity
and insecurities.

You opened up my heart,
and still held the door for me.
Allowed me to re-enter
uncomfortable
compartments of pain,
that I constantly dismissed
inside myself with great disdain.

You love me,
unconditionally.
And for you,
Dhanshaly Persaud,
I vow to do the same.

Love Resides

Love resides
in the crevices
of soft cuddles
sweet words
of reassurance
and everlasting laughter.

Love resides
in luminous eyes
revealing the depths
of our emotional chambers,
where inner beauty
is gently embedded.

Love resides
Beneath the surface,
Beyond our insecurities,
Intertwined,
Intensifying
Ignited passion
Burning relentlessly
Between our timeless souls.

Morning Kisses

Your morning kisses
travel gracefully,
while velvet palms awaken me.
Glide smoothly as a ballpoint pen,
I'm captivated by your zen.

Engulfed in your tranquility.
Lulled by your love,
still half asleep.
I rise to your majestic eyes.
Without a word,
your aura speaks.

From the light of my crown
to your warmth on my cheeks,
your kisses release
the Goddess in me.
Your butter-soft lips
melted in mine.
Our love transcends
confines of time.

The sacred bliss
of morning hours
is a preview of heaven
your presence empowers.
Awakened by your eternal affection,
God grants us divine protection.

Love Feels

Your love feels like the
cool satisfaction of silk
satin scarves on my
freshly washed scalp.

Your love feels like the
warmth and fuzziness of froth,
hot chocolate topped
with whipped cream
on a wintry night.

Your love feels like
the shadowy glow
at a candlelit dinner.
Inviting as soft jazz,
soft as your outstretched hand,
locked in mine across the table.

Your love feels,
Your love lives
infinitely between
time and space,
frozen still
but ever-flowing
interwoven,
our cosmic energy
magically
magnetically
pulling us closer,
lifting us higher
beyond the physical
inside the spiritual-
Your love is.

Her Infinite Love

We are cosmically aligned
and spiritually entwined.
Beyond romantically smitten,
our love is infinitely written.
Across the stars of abundance,
divine destinies glisten.
I honor and uphold your gifts
to heal, inspire and uplift.

Elevation is inescapable
in her divine presence.
Sacred hands resemble gold,
that hold her goddess essence.
An honor to explore her galaxy.
A perfect balance, your duality
of masculine and feminine energy
collide like astronomical entities.

Section Three

Grief

Grief is one of the most painful experiences we face, but it is not limited to the loss of physical life. Many times, we may grieve past versions of ourselves and those we love. Some relationships are inevitably lost, as we embark on our individual healing journeys. Just remember, your feelings are valid. Be kind and patient with yourself along this lonely road.

Sleep Peacefully Grandma

Sleep peacefully Grandma,
in God's most delicate skies.
Your distinctive smile and laughter,
I cherish and visualize.

Sleep peacefully Grandma,
you lived a plentiful life.
Took one breath and transcended,
without any pain or strife.

Sleep peacefully Grandma,
our spirits remain aligned.
On February 9th,
we honor you for all time.
Sleep peacefully Grandma,
despite death's devastation,
abundant memories of you
renew a joyous celebration.

Sleep peacefully Grandma.

Let It Go

The scars of grief
cut deep beneath,
but death is guaranteed.
May the tears you weep
sweep you into
waves of inner peace.

May your memories give solace,
when it's harder to accept.
Loss of life is only physical,
eternal souls are kept.

Please prioritize the present,
healing energy will flow.
Nothing on this earth
is ours to keep.
Love and let it go.

Growing Apart

Losing you while finding me
is the hardest place to be.
How did we plant the strongest seed,
then shy away from our own tree?
Our love's embedded in this soil,
but on the ground are falling leaves.
As we embrace our higher selves,
our disconnection is the fee.

A costly sacrifice in life
is letting go to be in flow.
We prayed for blossoms of abundance,
can't be surprised when flowers grow.

I love your vibe and frequency,
but maybe it collides with mine.
Seems we have
less and less in common,
catching trips to pass the time.

They say that opposites attract,
but is that really sustainable?
God put us on two greater paths,
so now you're unattainable.

I understand, won't hold you back
but where does love meet isolation?
I prayed to be of divine service,
no time to question elevation.

This ain't goodbye
This ain't no breakup
I stutter saying separation.
So do we call it intermission,
as we embark on lonely missions?

Why do we feel a sense of guilt
to follow faith and intuition?
When hummingbirds are set to fly,
they do not ask for one's permission.

I'm proud to see you soar, my Queen.
I hope that you remember home.
But just in case you need to know,
I love you and you're not alone.

Safe Space

Is there a safe space
for the creative
whose confidence
slowly chips away?
Energy drained
by mundane workdays,
for low pay and high bills
leave them no time to stray
into vast fields
of one's imagination.

How could we ever feel complacent
in a system that upholds the algorithm?
Amplifies the artificial,
as original art
bleeds and grieves-
a loss of pure passion,
lacking authenticity.
Bless the artist
whose creativity
is crafted from the soul.
Your breakthrough will be abundant,
every blessing will unfold.

Is there a home
for the healer
whose heart
has hairline cracks?
Although she shines,
she gently carries
minor wear and tear
because she loved
unconditionally,
but wasn't handled with care.

Find a safe space
in your heart
that unlocks eternal bliss.
Find a safe space
in your mind
where only peace and love exist.
May your safe space
be your bubble.
Let no trouble come your way.
May this safe space
keep you grounded
so your soul will never sway.

Painful Liberation

Grieving who you once were
reveals entrapment of the mind.
Shatter clocks of mental time.
Allow pure consciousness to shine.

Compulsive images of self
are gravely tainted by our thoughts.
You may grieve newfound success,
if you think happiness is bought.

Misunderstood by family members,
as you step into your greatness?
Pour compassion into their cups
that overflow with limitations.

You may mourn
withering friendships-
the expense of elevation.
Grief of past and present self
can be a painful liberation.

Section Four

Reflection

Sometimes looking back is the only way to move forward. I used to bury myself in shame for past mistakes, behaviors and coping mechanisms that I adopted in my unconscious state. The weight of guilt one carries is gravely embedded into their memories. When we internalize self-inflicted burdens, we are unable to ascend to elevated heights. We place anchors on our physical, mental, spiritual and emotional growth by harboring regret. As we look into the mirrors of our past, may we meet our reflections with compassion, not criticism. You are not defined by your mistakes. You are not unworthy of love, forgiveness and healing. Allow your experiences to shape and propel you beyond your own understanding. In every lesson, there is an opportunity to transcend into your higher self. Look back periodically, but please don't stay behind.

Look Deeper

What if you looked
deep inside yourself
and didn't recognize
what you see?

Changing the world
is an ambitious feat,
but transformation
starts with me.

What if you looked
deep inside yourself
and rejected
your soul's reflection?

God is within you,
look in the mirror.
Consciousness
is a divine connection.

Note to Self

Self-discovery
lies inside
mucky waters
of insecurity.

Self-love
is deciding
to abandon
self-neglect.

Self-care
cares less
about what
anybody thinks.

Self-worth
is immeasurable.
Fortify your
self-respect.

Cheers

Cheers to this version of you,
overwhelmed and uncelebrated.
Despite your own progress,
you're unsatisfied until you "make it."

Even when you've "made it,"
you hardly give yourself grace.
You won't find true happiness
with your virtues out of place.

Cheers to this version of you,
upholding societal expectations.
Untrustworthy of the process,
and quickly running out of patience.

Cheers to the ignorance,
disappointment,
and skeptical self-worth.
Will you celebrate yourself
if it's your last day on earth?

Pure Soul

I was working overtime
at micromanaging my mind.
I let the ego supervise,
so every thought was scrutinized.
Foolish lies I told myself,
thinking I was in control.
Until I got the ego fired,
by the pureness of my soul.

Little Reminders

I wrote myself a letter that said,
"Remember to be tender"
but I forgot to give myself some grace,
so it returned to sender.

This little letter reappeared
with consciousness enclosed.
I would've kept the message,
but my mailbox overflowed.

So, I wrote myself a note
that simply told me to "declutter."
My conscience slowly cleared
and then my heart began to flutter.

For after all these years,
I just allowed myself to be.
The less I held on to the mess,
the more I became free.

Section Five

Forgiveness

Oftentimes, we ask God for forgiveness, but how deeply do we forgive ourselves? Are we open and willing to forgive others? There is no one-size-fits-all or time schedule when it comes to forgiveness and healing. What seems like irreversible damage may take years for a broken heart to mend, even if the pieces were shattered by you. Why remain shackled to self-loathing, immobilized by blame? This isn't to justify wrongdoings or downplay their effects on you. You may forgive but never forget, and there is peace within that truth. The sooner we are able to forgive, the freer and lighter our spirits will be to transcend psychological time. We escape the mental loops of destructive memories, when we find the strength to forgive. Be gentle with yourself along this healing journey. Only you will know when it's time to release. Your heart is not a storage space to harbor resentment. Your heart is deserving of limitless, unconditional love.

Self-Forgiveness

The road to self-forgiveness
can be unsettling, unkind.
Unresolved, shameful thoughts
creep and consume
subconscious minds.

Buried shame resurfaces
from harsh words
I once uttered.
But holding on to self-blame,
only keeps your brain cluttered.

Stop cringing at past behavior
and do yourself this favor:

Forgive yourself.

The weight of guilt
isn't worth the heavy labor.

Oceans Deep

The rotten roots
of family trees
run oceans deep
with jealousy.

Who knew my angry aunt
would taunt me
with her lifelong misery?
Her words still haunt me,
"Dark and ugly"
ripped away my self-esteem.
As a child, although I smiled,
to feel her love was just a dream.

I forgive,
but still, I see
how she despises
my light beam.
Every time she's met with love,
she can't resist the urge to scream.
I learned the battle isn't personal,
she's fighting entities.
Please win the war within yourself
so there are no more casualties.
Your grandson has the brightest gleam.
Don't dim him down like you did me.
Broken hearts and childhood scars
create the perfect masterpiece.

I pray you heal what you don't speak.
I pray you learn what you don't teach.
I pray you find the love within
so that your soul no longer weeps.
No longer spewing hateful words,
unconscious talk is awfully cheap.
Accountability is key,
but jealousy
runs oceans deep.

Release Revenge

Emancipate your mind
from the impulse
to seek revenge.
A hardened heart
does more harm to you,
than it does to them.

Parental Expectations

Free yourself from the blame
you place on your parents.
Too stern? Not present?
No emotional connection?
Did you ever feel neglected?
Do those feelings softly linger?
Are you triggered in their presence?
Feel the urge to point the finger?

Amplified internal voices,
our inner child won't quiet down.
Will we forgive their imperfections,
if and when they're not around?

Do you mourn what could've been?
Secretly yearn for something more?
Do you seek heartfelt apologies
and love that's truly pure?
Reciprocation and appreciation
are all that you asked for.
Did they downplay your dreams
and your desire to explore?

Release the tendency to grieve
the life you knew that you deserved.
Allow the pain to flow freely,
when childhood trauma hits a nerve.
Pour the love you crave into yourself.
Trust,
you are deserving.
Look inside yourself and smile,
you are the one to break the curses.

My Mother's Keeper

Through my mother's eyes
are unrealized dreams.
Captured pictures,
but her smile
isn't really as it seems.
Printed photos
fully framed
but neglected by the dust.
Sometimes I wonder
if the little girl inside her
learned to trust.

Did she wrestle with self-love?
Did she struggle with self-care?

Sometimes I gaze into my mother's eyes
and wonder if she's there.
Drowning in monotony
but mentally, she's unaware.
Trapped in a loop
of faded memories,
while passing down her fears.

Beneath the echoes of her laughter
lies a sad and shallow void.
God forgive my own unconsciousness
each time I grow annoyed.
I feel her emptiness contagiously,
and yearn for something deeper.
She chooses to remain unkept,
but I will be my mother's keeper.

Subtle tingles in my heart,
but Mommy, I'll be by your side.
Pushing past my own discomfort,
to divorce my pain and pride.
Meeting you with more compassion,
loving unconditionally.
Nurturing my family tree,
breaking the cycle
starts with me.
I'll always be
My Mother's Keeper

Brighter Days

I got lost in my loneliness
and danced in my discomfort.
I missed a step then stumbled
on my own unconsciousness.

I lay and wept
and prayed for grace,
while dealing with temptation.
Distractions fly like darts,
targeting my elevation.

Went down rabbit holes to chase it,
but was met with low vibrations.
Silly rabbits of my sadness
only led to more bad habits.

Gambling and drinking wine
became the norm for idle time.
Losing money is the least,
when you misplace
your peace of mind.

Shriveled leaves of family trees
intensified my disconnection.
Within mirrors of their emptiness,
I saw my own reflection.

I ask God for redemption,
but I must redeem me first.
Where's the fountain of forgiveness
when you slowly die of thirst?
Where's the hunger for His Word?
Do we accept what we despise?
Reject systemic lies,
as we see Babylon's demise.

I pray the real ones rise,
by stepping out of our own way.
May we embrace the darkness
for The Light of brighter days.

Falling Short

I'm seeking light
in days of darkness,
trying to harness
higher vibrations.
Sometimes, my heart
and mind are divided
like a war between two nations.

On this journey
of truth and healing,
may my spirit
be in alignment.
God, I know You've given tests.
At times, I fail the assignment.

For the times I've fallen short,
thank You for Your love and grace.
Let my ego be uprooted,
take me to a conscious place.

On this quest
to find redemption,
cleanse my heart,
my mind and soul.
If true richness
comes from life,
may I find
eternal gold.

I Forgive Myself

I forgive myself
for every time
I acted out of spite.

I forgive myself
for days of rage
and countless
drunken nights.

I forgive myself
for hurtful words
I said but didn't mean.

I forgive myself
for brutal beatings
on my self-esteem.

I forgive myself
for guilt trips
that diluted my dreams.

I forgive myself
for vengeful thoughts
and calculated schemes.

I forgive myself
for hiding who
I always knew I was.
The men I let into my space
and dated "just because."

I apologize
for squinting eyes
when I saw my reflection.
The little girl I hurt inside
who needed my protection.

I apologize
when I deprive myself
of time and love,
that I expect from others.
Look inside to rise above.

I forgive myself today
because each day
I wake is borrowed.
To bask in everlasting joy,
I must relinquish sorrow.

I forgive myself

Section Six

Alignment

Each and every being has a divine assignment, but are we in alignment? Tapping into collective consciousness allows us to be aligned with God's Will and the Universal Laws. If you ever feel spiritually imbalanced, it may be time to starve the ego. Alignment unleashes eternal abundance.

Completely Me

Who told me that I was incomplete?
My own eyes were deceiving.
Years of searching for the missing pieces,
wrongfully believing,
I was never good enough.
Worried I was never whole.
Affection wasn't shown by family,
"I love you" was rarely told.

Who told me that I was incomplete?
And why did I agree?
Was it the ego's hurtful lies,
painfully disguised as me?
Years of frowning at my flaws,
wallowing in falsity,
leading me astray,
a vast array of insecurities.

Thank God, I finally see!
I was never incomplete.
I shine brilliantly,
abundantly blessed
and breaking free.
I have always held the keys
buried deep inside of me.
Gleaming gold inside this soul
is one whole beautiful, Black Queen.

Allow

I allow myself to feel the shift,
a transformation looming.
Storms must pass
and thunder cracks,
before a flower's blooming.

Transformation rarely comes
without waves of confusion.
If doubt scribbles in your mind,
do not quickly draw conclusions.

Allow joy and pain to coexist,
within your soul's infusion.
Why would you ever wait
on time to change,
if time is an illusion?

Soul Freedom

They say,
"A mind is a terrible thing to waste"
but what if you're wasting away
in your mind?
The more you internalize tricks that it plays,
you create a spiritually conscious decline.

How do we break free
from the prisons we built?
Mentally chained
to an ego ingrained.
The key is revealed
once you choose to be still.
Yet, stillness requires
transmuting the pain.

The tingling sense
of sadness you store,
invites negative energies
for your psyche to explore.
This grows into anger,
explodes into rage.
Release and let love
free your soul
from this cage.

The Other Side

Treading tumultuous waters
in my subconscious mind.
Swimming for dear life
to cross the other side,
where divine connections
and pure consciousness lie.
As new dimensions arise,
peaceful spirits will thrive.

Light as a feather
is the only way
we'll ever survive.
Light in heart
Light in mind
for love and light to align.
Please don't stay behind.

Today I Decided

Today I Decided
not to succumb
to meager crumbs
sprinkled carelessly
along strategic traps
keeping those
complacent
in the rat race.

Today I Decided
to intentionally
defy the hamster wheel.
I refuse to run in place,
stuck in society's pace.

Instead, I elevate
avoiding expectations
of aimless living.
Maneuvering this matrix,
I observe the simulation.

Today I Choose
to explore the greenery
of God's creations.
Therapeutically indulging
in Mother Nature's gifts.

Today I Choose
to inspire and uplift
your creative energy.
Intrinsically implanted
by His wisdom within.

Divine Alignment

God,
thank You
for blessing me
with a purposeful life.
Mending my heart of pain
and self-inflicted strife.

Thank you to my ancestors,
guiding me as light beams.
Every single tear you cried
provides divine streams
of generational wealth,
to break generational curses.
I live out your wildest dreams
in every country that I surface.

I surrender to your presence, God.
I'm blessed to be of service,
to You and only You.
Please use me for a greater purpose.

If my judgment's ever cloudy,
if past behaviors reappear,
if I feel a chill of loneliness,
remind me that You're near.

Wrapping me in His divinity,
our energies unfold.
Aligning mind and spirit,
healing my eternal soul.

God's Glory

Why did I tippy-toe to greatness?
Too afraid of my own story.
Bottled emotions left me frozen.
I was chosen by God's glory.

Standing here as living proof
of urgent times to save the youth.
If you need hope to cling onto,
then take His hand and walk in truth.

Let God lead you to that peace
that seems so hard to find inside.

Let God feed you with His words
so you no longer choke on pride.

Let God lift you from your prison-
mentally, spiritually.
We see the world's at war with entities.
Let us stay strapped in sanctity.

God, please break down these blockages
that keep us worldly-bound.

God is moving mountains we don't see,
so stand on solid ground.

Let God's glory tell your story.
In His wisdom, we are found.

Cause if we weaponize our words,
we amplify unconscious sounds.

God is Glorious

Section Seven

Elevation

Congratulations for embarking on this courageous journey to healing and elevation. If you haven't begun, the very act of opening your heart and mind to *Eternally You* is a powerful start. You are more than capable of doing the inner work by indulging in nature, practicing stillness, reflection, self-love, forgiveness and more. Take pride in this conscious effort of aligning your mind, body and spirit in positive ways. You are doing amazing things leading up to your spiritual enlightenment. It's only a matter of time before you find your higher purpose and reach the pinnacle of divine elevation.

Egyptian Elevation

Evidence of who I am
adorns this ancient, sacred land.
Retracing steps where it began,
the richness of our history stands.
Filled with pride since I've arrived,
my blackness beams on scorching sands.
Mesmerized by Giza Pyramids,
we've made it to the Motherland!

As I comb through Cairo streets,
my braids sway in this desert heat.
Recognized by warm, Egyptian eyes,
they smile and greet: a Nubian Queen.
Addressing me, affectionately
as royalty, "Nefertiti!"
Enchanted by my chocolate skin,
they know the truth of melanin.

Still, I cannot help but think-
who shot the nose off of this Sphinx?
The sun sets as our camels trot,
I wonder if they need a drink.

We cruise in style along The Nile.
Egyptian love makes me at home.
I witness true black royalty,
including King Tut's mask and throne.
I humbly stand inside his tomb,
in the Valley of the Kings.
As we peruse through each cartouche,
the walls of Hieroglyphics sing.
Colossal statues strongly prove,
Black excellence is what we bring.

Leap of Faith

Lately, I've been feeling
an unsettling sensation.
My higher self awaits
my leap of faith
in contemplation.
Slowly growing
clearly showing
agitation and frustration.
Lucid dreams of being free
plague my presence
in workspaces.
Punching clocks
like auction blocks,
keep us shackled
in the matrix.
Am I running toward my destiny
or running out of patience?

My heart and mind unfasten.
My legs strengthen for the jump.
My faith in God will guide me
out of this systemic slump.
Songs of freedom
pull my heartstrings,
I must liberate myself.
Instead of placing keys to freedom
in the hands of someone else.

Fellow leapers on the ledge,
does the journey
make you nervous?
Are you doubtful of the process,
worried that you don't deserve this?
To escape career captivity
fearlessly,
pursue your purpose.
Take the greatest leap of faith;
God, how can I be of service?

Self-Discovery

Make time
for the deepest desires
of your heart,
unwillingly tucked away
by tiresome work days.

Shine light
on your sensational
talents and thoughts.
Overshadowed by self-doubt,
needing approval from others.

Free yourself
from the urge
to seek external validation.
Truth is,
they don't care as much
as you think they do.

Create space
for the real you.
Eternally you.
The purest form
of self-love
is at the verge
of self-discovery.

Lonely Road

Elevation is a lonely road.

You may stumble upon resentment
while mourning lost friendships.
Cradling underlying tension.
Incomprehension
leads to disconnection.

Family may not recognize you.
Some may start to despise you.
Allow the Most High to guide you.

Some strangers who cross your path
may gravitate to drain your energy.
Stay clear of subtle enemies,
light dimmers carry envy.

The highest road is walked alone.
Navigate through low vibrations.
Your lonesome path is built to last.
Thank God for elevation.

Mind Elevation

Old habits keep us confined
mindlessly to aged routines.
If we remain in a sleep state,
we may not realize our dreams.

Subconscious dreams of being free
may seem harder to obtain.
Instead of running from this challenge,
learn to rewire your brain.
The most powerful muscle
every human being must train.
Wash away monotonous living,
spark new habits to maintain.
Like a seasoned investor,
seeking out the greatest gains
on this risky road to growth,
may no losses go in vain.

Some may not believe your journey.
Some may not perceive your pain.
Some may not receive your reasoning,
Some may think you've gone insane.

Worry none,
elevation is the vital evolution.

May you find spiritual clarity,
to cleanse worldly confusion.
May you listen more intuitively,
resist the outside noise.
May you overcome your blockages,
accentuate your inner voice.
May you give yourself grace
and unconditional self-love.
May you heal your inner child,
so he or she will rise above.

You will transcend to new levels.
You will find your higher purpose.
You will thrive in your alignment.
Stubborn habits will not serve us.
You will dwell in endless joy.
You will finally feel free.
All the answers I was searching for
reside inside of me!

Made in the USA
Columbia, SC
16 February 2025